HOW TO PROTECT YOUNG PEOPLE AGAINST SEXUAL ABUSE AND RISKY SEXUAL BEHAVIORS

HOW TO PROTECT YOUNG PEOPLE AGAINST SEXUAL ABUSE AND RISKY SEXUAL BEHAVIORS

Parents who expose their children to sexual abuse are as culpable as the perpetrators.

Find out 62 ways young people are exposed to sexual abuse and risky sexual behaviors.

Learn 55 ways to protect your wards against sexual abuse and risky sexual behaviors

ROSEMARY OSHIOMAH OGEDENGBE

To order additional copies of this book, contact:
Xlibris Corporation
1-888-795-4274
www.Xlibris.com
Orders@Xlibris.com
109908

Contents

DEDICATION

To the Almighty God, the lifter up of my head and to all children.

PREFACE

Many unsuspecting young boys and girls have been sexually abused by caregivers who turned out to be paedophiles. These include relations, family friends, teachers, religious leaders, neighbours, and parents in some cases. Also, many young people have become sexually permissive. Incest, homosexual relationship, masturbation and prostitution are common among today's children and adolescents. The physiological, psychological, spiritual as well as the socio-economic consequences of this trend on the individual, the family and the society are grievous.

Hence, parental intervention is imperative. This book, "How to Protect Young People Against Sexual Abuse and Risky Sexual Behaviors" is designed to equip parents and caregivers with the knowledge and skills that they need in order to protect young people against sexual abuse and harmful sexual behaviors.

The book contains seven chapters. Chapter one is a documentary on the incidence of sexual abuse of minors in Nigeria. Chapter two provides insight into the meaning and forms of sexual abuse and how it is perpetrated. It also presents tips that would assist parents to identify potential perpetrators of sexual abuse. Chapter three is a presentation of the victim in a situation of sexual abuse. It highlights the experience, consequences, indications, and risk factors of sexual abuse as well as the assistance that could be rendered to the victim. Chapter four presents an overview of risky sexual behaviors among young people as well as the signs that are suggestive of a child's involvement in sexual activities.

Chapter five is a discussion of the risk factors and causes of sexual abuse and risky sexual behaviors among young people, while chapter six highlights the measures that could be taken to protect young people against sexual abuse and risky sexual behaviours as well as how to help a child who is involved in risky sexual behaviours. Chapter seven which is the last chapter deals with questions which relate to young people's sexuality as well as the answers.

The author's choice of the use of the feminine pronoun "she" is based on the belief that females are more vulnerable to sexual abuse than males.

Parents, teachers, counselors and other caregivers would find this book helpful in their provision of guidance and protection for young people against sexual abuse and risky sexual behaviors.

Rosemary Oshiomah Ogedengbe.

ACKNOWLEDGEMENT

I am grateful to God Almighty for His unfailing love, and to the Holy Spirit, my personal tutor and counselor.

I will forever be indebted to my lecturers at the university of Lagos; Dr. Sola Aletan, Dr. M. B. Ubangha, Dr. Awoyifa, Prof. Ngozi Osarenren, Prof. Mopelola Omoegun, Prof. A. M. Olusakin, Prof. P.B. Ikulayo, Prof. G. C. Ilogu, Dr C.E Okoli, my post graduate course adviser who also supervised my undergraduate research work, Dr. B. O. Makinde, my undergraduate course adviser and Dr. I.P. Nwadinigwe who supervised my post graduate research work.

I acknowledge the contributions of my friends; Balaraba Idoko, Rena Osemuahu, Grace Ejime, Ihuoma Isaac, Uche Dimgba and Wale Taiwo.

To Doris, Raymond and Jude, thanks for your love.

I am also thankful to my mum, Mrs. Juliana Okhifo and my siblings; Joachim, Felix, Emmanuel, Faith, Joy, Esther and Grace for their love and encouragement.

To my aunt, Mrs. P.F. Agba, I will forever remember your contributions.

Exceedingly worthy of my appreciation are my children; Naomi, Perfect, Fortune and Victor for their cooperation and love.

To the love of my life, Oshiomah Ogedengbe, thank you for your love and support.

To my spiritual parents; Bishop and Rev Mrs. John Osa-Oni, Bishop and Rev. Mrs. O.K Inyang and the entire ministers of Vineyard Christian Ministries, thank you for helping me to discover my purpose and potentials.

CHAPTER ONE

IS THE SEXUAL ABUSE OF MINORS A MYTH OR A REALITY?

"My grandmother is willing to take care of me, but she said she doesn't want the baby. So for now, I can't go back home to my relatives until the government takes this baby off my hands".

Those were the words of 14years old Kehinde who was delivered of a child which resulted from incessant sexual abuse by her father. (Saturday Punch, Dec. 11, 2010)

The sexual abuse of children is a menace which is becoming increasingly prevalent in our society. Inspite of the fact that most cases of sexual abuse are often swept under the carpet especially in this part of the world, evidences of the prevalence of the calamity abound. A report by the Iranian News Agency IRIN in January 2008, quoting the Police and Kano State government officials, said that 54 cases of child rape were recorded in the state within six months in 2007. According to the report, the victims were girls aged 3-11years, one of whom was raped to death.

In April 2010, neighbors caught a 65year old man as he attempted to defile a 2year old infant in Aremo area of Ibadan.

In May 2010, a man who claimed to be an Islamic cleric was accused by the police in Surulere, Lagos, of raping a 14 year old girl whom he kept in Akute, Ogun state.

In July 2010, a 21year old boy was detained at Alade police station in Lagos for allegedly raping two girls of the same parents aged 6 and 9 in Onipanu.

In August 2010, a 60year old man was arraigned in a magistrate court in Osun state for allegedly raping a 13year old girl in Otokobo community.

In the same August 2010, a 48year old sailor was arrested for raping his 2year old infant daughter. The report noted that he had penetrated her at least four times and that he had been violating her since she was a year old.

(The Punch News Paper, August 8, 2010.)

In November 2010, a 7year old Mfon was brutally abused by a neighbour in Calabar, Crossriver. The same disaster befell Muibat, a 10year old who bled for hours after an ordeal with her neighbor in Ijeshatedo, Surulere, Lagos.

(Sunday Sun, Nov. 28, 2010.)

These evidences point to the fact that there are more pedophiles amongst us than we can imagine. It is therefore imperative for us as parents to take the protection of our children very seriously.

CHAPTER TWO

WHAT PARENTS SHOULD KNOW ABOUT THE SEXUAL ABUSE OF MINORS

WHAT REALLY IS SEXUAL ABUSE?

The word "abuse" generally means the wrongful use of a thing, place or person. Sexual abuse is the wrongful use of an individual by another for sexual gratification.

SEXUAL ABUSE OCCURS IN DIFFERENT FORMS

The sexual abuse of children can occur in different forms. Reisser, Cox and Wright (1997) classified the sexual abuse of children into two forms:

- Sexual Contact
- Sexual Interaction

Sexual Contact:—This involves any form of physical intimacy with a child, with the intention to achieve sexual arousal or gratification of the perpetrator, or to arouse the child, irrespective of whether the perpetrator's intention is to sensitize the child in order to gain further sexual gratification or not. It also involves any deliberate contact with a child's genitals or erotic areas without genuine reasons, such as medical reasons, irrespective of whether the contact is meant to produce sexual stimulation or not. Examples of sexual contacts are:

- Direct genital contact—This refers to penetrative intercourse which could be anal, oral or vaginal penetration which is commonly referred to as rape. Rape is defined by the section 357 of the Nigerian criminal code as *"having unlawful carnal knowledge of a woman or a girl without her consent, or with her consent if the consent is obtained by force or by means of threat or intimidation of any kind or by fear of harm or by means of false and fraudulent representation as to the nature of the act, or in the case of a married woman, by impersonating her husband"*.

- Sexual contact also refers to the manipulation of the erotic areas of a victim, such as fondling or kissing of the lips, breasts, genitals, neck, stomach, ears, upper arm, thighs, navel, anus, buttocks and waist whether such areas are covered or uncovered.

Sexual Interaction: Sexual interactions do not involve physical touch or contact with a child; rather, they are activities that are often orchestrated with the intention to gain sexual arousal of some sort from the child, or to lure her into more intimate sexual relations. Such interactions include:

- *Visual Interaction*—This involves the exposure of a child to sexually explicit materials such as pornographic videos or literature, or the deliberate exposure of the perpetrator's genitals to the child in order to gain sexual arousal or the intentional viewing of a child's nudity for pleasure.
- *Verbal Interaction*—Verbal interaction involves the use of language or statements which suggest sexual intentions. An example of this is when a man involves a child in discussions that are focused on sexual activities.

Sexual Interaction also occurs when an adult involves a child in his or her personal sexual concerns. Here, the intention is neither to arouse the child nor to gain personal sexual stimulation but to confide in the child. For instance, an ignorant single parent may erroneously share their difficulties in sexual relationships with their adolescent of the same sex, without being aware of the psychological impact of such discussions on the child.

Same Sex Abuse

Same sex abuse occurs when an individual forces another person of the same sex to participate in sexual activities.

The Saturday Punch (Jan 15, 2011) reported the story of a 17year old boy who was sexually abused by a 29year old "homosexual" in Oshogbo. As more people become involved in homosexual relationship, same sex abuse is also likely to become common. An individual who is homosexual has the tendency to lure younger ones of the same sex into sexual relations. Parents therefore need to be on guard. If you suspect any unwholesome interaction between your child and someone of the same sex, it would be wise to investigate the situation. Those that we need to watch out for include:

- An adult who does not show interest in relationship with people of the opposite sex.
- An adult who enjoys intimate relationship with far younger children of the same sex instead of adults.
- Anyone who is morally porous.
- An individual with a record of homosexual behavior.
- An individual who behaves more like people of the opposite sex. An example is a male who dresses and talks like a female.
- Anyone who speaks in favour of homosexual relationship.
- An individual who expresses sexual admiration towards persons of the same sex.
- An adult who seems not to experience physical attraction to persons of the opposite sex—He may experience such feelings towards persons of the same sex.
- Anyone who has been sexually abused by someone of the same sex.
- Individuals who are bi-sexual—They are capable of maintaining sexual relations with people of the same sex as well as those of the opposite sex. These homosexuals are more difficult to identify.

Who is Vulnerable to Same Sex Abuse?

Children who are in the boarding and those who attend single sex schools are very much at risk because older students who are already sexually active but are now restricted by the school environment may resort to homosexual relationships and the younger ones are usually the "preys". Also, those who have been sexually abused by people of the same sex may pick on younger ones of the same sex and abuse them. Other children who are equally vulnerable are those who possess the physical characteristics of the opposite sex. For example, a young boy who is so handsome to the point of being mistaken for a girl would be attractive to a male-male homosexual who seeks a male-female, while a girl who has a masculine frame would be attractive to a lesbian who seeks a female-male. Children who are exposed to homosexuals either directly or through the media are also vulnerable. It is important to note that same sex abuse is not less dehumanizing. Hence, we need to be watchful.

WHEN A GROWN VIRGIN IS VIOLENTLY ABUSED

A grown girl who has preserved her virginity only for it to be forcefully taken away from her would definitely experience a greater loss and become far more traumatized than a victim who had been sexually active. Therefore, being able to ascertain a victim's sexual status before the abuse would help to determine the kind and depth of assistance which should be rendered to the victim.

BOYS CAN ALSO BE ABUSED BY FEMALES

Parents often lose sight of the fact that male children also need to be protected against sexual exploitation. There had been cases where under aged boys were lured into sexual activities by older females. The sexual abuse of a boy child poses no less danger than that of a girl.

Sexual intercourse is not a mere physical activity; it is a deep physical interaction with physiological, emotional, psychological, social and spiritual implications which are too complex for a child to comprehend.

HOW IS SEXUAL ABUSE PERPETRATED?

Sexual abuse involves the assertion of some sort of "force" or power by the assailant on the victim. The power asserted could be physical—where the culprit is physically stronger and uses physical force which may include the use of weapons such as knives, guns or acid to subdue the victim.

In some situations, the assailant uses emotional and intellectual manipulation, in which case he deceitfully uses his intellectual experience, verbal and other subtle skills such as soothing statements and token gifts to persuade the child to succumb to his wishes. Younger children between the ages of 2-13 and those who are mentally challenged are usually the ones who easily fall prey to this method. The gifts serve as positive reinforcement to the child, and make it difficult for her to realize that she is being abused.

A perpetrator may apply psychological influence on a victim. There are certain people in our lives to whom we find it difficult to say no. This situation is what exists between children and their parents, favourite older siblings, uncles, aunts, nannies and sometimes family friends. In such a situation, the perpetrator does not need to use any physical force neither does he require much persuasion to obtain the victim's cooperation since he already has enough psychological influence over her.

A perpetrator may also use his economic importance in the child's life as a weapon to enforce his wishes. For instance, it is difficult for a child or an adolescent to say no to a man who feeds her or pays her school fees.

Some perpetrators apply religious manipulations. There have been cases of young people who were abused by their pastors, Imams or Sunday school teachers. Religious manipulation involves the perpetrator's application of religious injunctions such as *"Obey your parents in the Lord"*, to psychologically compel the child to comply. Besides this, children who are very religious usually hold their spiritual leaders in high esteem and look up to them as spiritual role models and would therefore not suspect immorality in what they do. Some children have been abused by their spiritual leaders under the pretence of helping them to ward off evil spirits or pending dangers.

WHO ARE THE PERPETRATORS OF SEXUAL ABUSE AND HOW CAN WE IDENTIFY THEM?

With the high incidence of child abuse discussed earlier, bearing in mind that most of the incidents were perpetrated by close relations and other trusted persons, the beginning of wisdom if you really want to ensure the safety of your child is to regard everyone as a potential culprit. This may sound very harsh, but to whom can we entrust our innocent daughters in an era when teachers, uncles, aunts and even parents violate little children?

It is impossible to read anyone's mind, but certain behaviours could be pointers to hidden motives and tendencies. Hence, you need to watch out for anyone who does the following:

1. Enjoys bullying.
2. Visits in your absence irrespective of whether they are of the opposite sex or not. Someone of the same sex can also abuse a child.
3. Gives gifts to your child and would not want you to be aware of such gifts.
4. Gives sensitive gifts such as bras, pants, boxers, and perfumes to your adolescent especially if they are of the opposite sex.
5. Makes passes at your adolescent or makes sexually suggestive statements about them.
6. Enjoys being alone with your child or adolescent without genuine reasons.

7. Enjoys watching your child naked.
8. Deliberately exposes their bodies especially the sensitive parts to your child or adolescent.
9. Has a record of sexual abuse as a perpetrator or as a victim.
10. Exhibits permissiveness.
11. Indulges in pornography.
12. Has a mental challenge.
13. Has difficulty in maintaining stable heterosexual relationship with people of same age, e.g. a man or a woman who has divorced severally or one who has remained unmarried after a long period of separation from the spouse.
14. Lacks moral principles.
15. Criticizes your child or adolescent always—He may be trying to cover up something or get back at the child for not cooperating.
16. Visits your child or adolescent in school without your consent or request for such assistance.
17. Accuses your adolescent of seduction—He may have sexually harassed her or have the intention to do so.
18. Anyone whom your child avoids may be doing something unpleasant to the child. Find out what it is.

The fact that an individual exhibits any of these behaviours does not out rightly imply that the person is a culprit, rather, it is a sign that you need to keep a watchful eye on such a person.

If anyone makes a suspicious move around your child, you have the right to investigate, ask questions, demand for clarification or confront the individual if the situation demands it. No matter how much you trust anyone, it is wise to always take the pains to verify your trust.

If the wellbeing of our children is really important to us, we should be ready to protect them at all costs. No one should be a sacred cow.

CHAPTER THREE

THE VICTIM IN THE SITUATION

THE NATURE AND EXPERIENCE OF SEXUAL ABUSE

Sexual abuse, particularly when direct genital contact (rape) is involved, is extremely traumatic in nature. Of all the inhuman treatments that could be meted out to an individual, "rape" is only comparable with murder. It is actually the murder of "personhood" because it destroys the victim psychologically while her biological frame remains. Sexual abuse inflicts pain, shame, helplessness and horror on the victim.

Sexual abuse is a form of bereavement because it causes the victim to lose her self—worth and dignity, and thereby causes unimaginable grief.

Like other traumatic experiences, sexual abuse is a painful and horrifying experience which leaves the victim with a persistent re-experience of the abuse through flash backs, reminiscence and nightmares, with the consequence that the horror, pain, anxiety, depression, shame, self pity and other painful emotions which originally accompanied the abuse are re-experienced by the victim.

Sexual abuse is an unlawful exploitation of the victim. Where physical force or threats are employed by the perpetrator, the victim's compliance is compelled through intimidation which results to the victim's feeling of loss of power and control, and this generates a feeling of helplessness which is worsened by the fact that most victims are neither able to avenge themselves, nor access the desired justice especially in a society such as Nigeria where a girl could be stigmatized for reporting an incident of sexual abuse.

Sexual abuse is degrading to the victim. It makes a mockery of the value, worth, respect and confidence which the individual has ever ascribed to herself and consequently deflates her self-esteem.

Sexual abuse, especially "rape", is a violent attack on the physical personality of the victim. It tramples on her right to the ownership and control of her body and her socio-personal boundaries. When the sexual abuse of a child becomes an ongoing activity, as it is in situations where the child lives with or has regular contact with the assailant, it amounts to a nightmare from which the child cannot wake up.

WHAT REINFORCES THE TRAUMA OF SEXUAL ABUSE?

The trauma of sexual abuse is basically maintained by two factors; silence and reminiscence.

How Does Silence Reinforce Trauma?

When we find the opportunity to share our burdens and hurts, we often experience some emotional relief irrespective of whether the person we have shared with has the capability to provide the desired solution or not. The opportunity to unburden deep seated hurts is therapeutic in itself and marks the beginning of emotional healing. However, sexual abuse is a deep-seated hurt which the individual ought to share but feels compelled to conceal.

Why Do Victims Conceal Their Abuse?

Many victims of sexual abuse live with the trauma for years without mentioning their experiences to anyone. This silence is maintained because of several reasons which include:

1. The fear of breaking the oath of allegiance which the child may have been compelled to take by the assailant.
2. Many perpetrators of sexual abuse usually make threats of maiming or killing their victims if they reveal their experiences.
3. The fear of stigmatization especially in a society where victims are sometimes blamed for their predicaments.
4. A victim may keep silent as a result of resentment towards the caregivers (parents or guardians) especially if she feels that the abuse was caused by their negligence.
5. The fear that the required justice would not be achieved even if one reports the event.
6. The fear that one might be doubted especially when the abuser is a respected member of the society.
7. The fear of the effects the news might have on other family members especially when the culprit is a respected member of the family, such as the victim's father, stepfather or guardian.

8. The fear that the report of the incident may pose a threat to one's survival particularly if the culprit happens to be the victim's only source of sustenance.

9. The fear that talking about the incident could re-awaken painful memories. Most victims maintain silence for this reason. They wish they could blot out the painful memories by keeping quiet, ironically, the more they keep quiet, the deeper they sink into depression.

The Reminiscence of Sexual Abuse is as Painful as the Actual Abuse.

We all wish we could forget about our painful experiences because of the hurts, bitterness and sometimes the depression, which the memories of such experiences bring to us. Sexual abuse is a soul rending experience which the victim earnestly desires to forget but which persistently re-surfaces through excruciating memories. Unfortunately, sexual abuse is an experience which leaves many cues. For instances, the appearance of the perpetrator as well as his smell never leave, his voice and statements continue to re-echo even years after the experience, the place of the abuse becomes frightening while the time of the year when the abuse took place becomes a season of nightmare for the victim. One victim lamented, "I sometimes fail to remember my birthday, but I've never missed that month and the day". As at the time this statement was made, the victim had lived with this painful memory for eleven years.

Even the clothes, body cream and perfume worn by the victim during the incident become associated with the experience. The memories of sexual abuse are as real as the actual abuse because they cause a re-experience of the abuse through nightmares and flashbacks. This re-experience generates in the individual both physical and psychological stress which are as painful as those experienced during the actual abuse. This is why it is often said, that "once a man abuses a woman, he abuses her for life". The memories live on. Sexual abuse is a life long injury.

THE CONSEQUENCES OF SEXUAL ABUSE ON THE VICTIM ARE DEVASTATING

Sexual abuse has physiological, emotional, psychological, social and spiritual consequences which are detrimental to the individual's wellbeing and development.

The Physiological Consequences.

The physiological effects include pain, injuries, and sexually transmitted diseases which include HIV/AIDS, warts, Herpes, Chlamydia, Gonorrhea, Syphilis and Pelvic Inflammatory Diseases (PID). An unplanned pregnancy may also result. Saliu (2009) reported that 5% of victims of sexual abuse become pregnant, 50% of the pregnancies are aborted and 6% of the victims who keep their pregnancies put their babies up for adoption. Abortion complications and sterility could result from the damage of the child's tender reproductive organs. Under aged girls (those who are less than 18years) who become pregnant are highly exposed to the risk of developing Vesicle Vaginal Fistula (VVF) as well as having still births. Early exposure to sexual intercourse has also been listed as one of the risk factors for cervical cancer. While some people may be murdered by their perpetrators, others may hate their bodies to the point of self-mutilation or suicide.

What are the Psychological Consequences?

The major psychological consequence of sexual abuse on the victim is trauma. Trauma is a psychological condition that is caused by severe shock. It is characterized by feelings of anxiety, fear, torment and helplessness. A person who is traumatized may feel isolated in a world of pain, horror and torment.

Some Psychologists such as Burgress and Lytle (1972) described trauma which results from sexual abuse as Rape Trauma Syndrome (RTS). According to them, a rape victim experiences trauma in two phases; the acute and the reorganization phases. The acute phase involves responses such as flashbacks, nightmares, anxiety, guilt, shame as well as denial and attempts to disconnect self from the reality of the abuse while the reorganization phase involves the victim's conscious attempt to put the abuse behind and reintegrate self into normal functioning, though the memories of the abuse and feelings of shame, insecurity, fear and low self-esteem may still remain. Unfortunately, many victims are never able to move from the acute phase to this second phase without help.

A worse situation known as Post Traumatic Stress Disorder (PTSD) may result from trauma. The Diagnostic and Statistical Manual of Mental Disorders IV defines Post traumatic Stress

Disorder as the development of characteristic symptoms following an exposure to an extremely traumatic stress involving direct personal experience of an event that involves actual or threatened death, or serious injury or threat to one's physical integrity or witnessing an event that involves death, injury or threat to the physical integrity of another person or learning about an unexpected or violent death, serious harm or threat of death or injury experienced by a family member or other close associates. The person's response to the event involves intense fear, horror, helplessness and disorganized or agitated behavior. The characteristic symptoms include:

- Continuous experiencing of the trauma through flashbacks, recollections and nightmares.
- Experience of a "numbing" of general responses to, or avoidance of stimuli associated with the trauma, dissociation, amnesia (loss of memory), withdrawal and general loss of interest and enthusiasm.
- Experience of ongoing symptoms of increased arousal such as insomnia (sleep difficulty), difficulty in concentration, hyper vigilance, anger outburst and exaggerated startled response.

Post traumatic stress disorder is a major threat to the mental health of the victim which usually requires clinical assistance.

The more the violence involved in an abuse, the more traumatized the victim would be. Examples of violent abuse include those which involve threats with guns, or other dangerous weapons, as well as verbal harassment, such as those perpetrated by armed robbers.

Another thing that can make a victim to be extremely traumatized is when a violent abuse is experienced on a continuous basis. This happens in a situation where the victim lives with the perpetrator or has regular contact with him, or where different people repeatedly abuse her.

A child victim may not experience immediate trauma if the abuse is perpetrated through deceit and persuasion. However, the child may later become traumatized as she grows up and begins to understand the implication of what she has experienced.

What are the Emotional Consequences?

The emotional consequences of sexual abuse include depression, loneliness, guilt, a feeling of limitation, hostility, anger outburst, mood swings, shame, anxiety, fear of places, events, persons and seasons associated with the abuse, self pity, self rejection and hysteria (a condition in which a person experiences extreme and uncontrollable emotions usually as a result of shock, the person may begin to cry or laugh in a wild manner).

Another Psychological consequence of sexual abuse is that it creates identity problem for the victim. It erodes the four pillars of identity which are being (effective existence), "past", "present", and "future". The victim's effective existence is hampered, her past becomes a nightmare such that she wishes she had no past, her present is rendered unbearable and she perceives her future as meaningless.

Other psychological effects of sexual abuse include helplessness, loss of power and control, distorted self concept and low self esteem, loss of self confidence, suspicion and suicide attempts.

Sexual abuse has Social consequences.

Social interaction aids emotional therapy. When we are in our low times, one of the ways we often rejuvenate is by interacting with others. However, this is not so for a victim of sexual abuse. The individual feels unprotected, unappreciated and unwanted and therefore withdraws herself. This self isolation generates deeper feelings of alienation and worsens the victim's state of depression.

Some victims resort to substance abuse as an escape from the painful emotional and psychological consequences of the abuse or as an attempt to cushion the loneliness which results from the absence of social interaction.

Sexual abuse especially when it occurs in childhood causes generalized suspicion and insecurity and thereby inhibits the individual's capability to sustain meaningful interpersonal relationship especially with the opposite sex and this can lead to difficulty in future mate selection.

Sexual abuse especially "Rape" is an assassination of the victim's sexuality. This is so because it impresses on the victim, a perverted concept of sexuality, rubs her of her right to sexual consent as well as her right to future sexual fulfillment by causing resentment and phobia for sexual relations. All these can lead to frigidity and inability to derive satisfaction from sexual relations in future marriage and jeopardize the individual's family life.

Sexual abuse causes distortion of body image as well as sexual role confusion which can make the victim to become vulnerable to sexual pervasions such as lesbianism, prostitution, nymphomania (addiction to sexual intercourse or insatiable desire to have sexual intercourse), masturbation and sadomasochism (a condition in which one derives pleasure from hurting the partner and being hurt during sexual relations).

What Does a Child that is Sexually Abused Give Back to the Society?

A child that is sexually abused is a potential danger to the society.

The calamity generated by the sexual abuse of minors ultimately rests on the society. A child's perception of the society and consequently their attitude to it as they grow up is a reflection of the feelings communicated to them. If a child is treated with love, affection appreciation and regards, he learns to also treat others in the same way, but if he is treated with cruelty, hostility and disdain, he also learns to express the same feelings towards others. When children are abused, they develop tendencies of cruelty, violence, insensitivity and hostility, which as they grow up may be expressed through vandalism, terrorism, armed robbery, prostitution, murder and abuse of others. The Sunday punch (Dec. 5, 2010) reported the story of an 11year old girl who buried her aunt's 18months old baby alive in Aboru, a suburb in Lagos. This girl may not have been sexually abused, but there is no doubt that she had not enjoyed adequate nurturing as a child. A child who is exposed to unbearable cruelty would naturally develop an insensitive attitude towards others, especially if they have a drive to get back at the society.

An individual who is sexually abused especially as a child develops the tendency to also sexually abuse others. In an interview with the Saturday Punch (Jan. 9, 2010), Princess Kayode; a care giver of sexual abuse victims, reported the case of an eight year old girl whose sexual urge was awakened through sexual abuse. The implication of this is that the girl may introduce other children into the act of sexual intercourse in order to satisfy her urge.

DOES SEXUAL ABUSE HAVE EDUCATIONAL AND ECONOMIC CONSEQUENCES?

The attendant physiological, emotional, social and psychological effects of sexual abuse impair the victim's mental and physical functioning with the result that her academic performance and general productivity significantly dwindle.

The victim's future may be marred by such immediate consequences as an unplanned pregnancy, disrupted educational development and emotional disturbance. Where injuries, sexually transmitted diseases and serious psychiatric problems results, huge sum of money would inevitably be expended by the victim or her family. This can impoverish the victim and her family.

WHAT ARE THE RISK FACTORS FOR THE CHILD?

There are several factors, conditions and situations that can make a child or an adolescent to become vulnerable to sexual abuse. These factors include:

- Lack of parental supervision
- Exposure of a child to surrogate parents such as stepfathers, stepmothers, uncles, aunts, distant relations or family friends.
- Many boarding school operators lack monitoring and supervision expertise and this exposes children to abuse by older students.
- Child labor—street hawking or the employment of a child as a domestic servant.
- Mental illness—a child that is mentally challenged can easily be manipulated.
- Failure to provide for the child—a child who is hungry may eat anywhere and a child who is homeless may take shelter anywhere.
- A young person who lacks assertiveness can easily be abused.
- Leaving a child in school after school hours endangers the child.
- When a child is orphaned or motherless, he/she lives at the mercy of others and is exposed to various forms of cruelty and abuse.

- When a child's parent abuses drug or alcohol, they are incapable of looking after the child and capable of abusing her.
- When a child is deprived of affection, acceptance, belongingness, attention and love, she desperately yearns for them and becomes an easy prey to anyone who offers them.
- High risk environments such as bars, restaurants and hotels expose children to sexual abuse.
- When a child's parent is mentally challenged, they cannot look adequately after the child and such a parent may also abuse the child.
- Early maturity—children who attain puberty earlier than expected are at risk of sexual abuse because they are physically mature and attractive to the opposite sex, while intellectually and emotionally, they are still children. Predators can easily take advantage of them if they are not adequately protected.
- Children who lack intimate parent-child interactions often lack the courage to discuss issues that bother on sexuality with their parents, therefore, they do not tell their parents when passes are being made at them. Consequently, they lack access to the parental guidance that should ordinarily help them to deal with such situations.
- A child who is materialistic can easily be lured with gifts.
- A child who has low self esteem can easily fall prey to anyone who makes her to feel important.
- A lazy child, who always depends on others to do her tasks, may have to pay in kind someday.

HOW WOULD A PARENT KNOW IF A CHILD HAS BEEN SEXUALLY ABUSED?

The experience of sexual abuse can be concealed by a child or an adolescent for many years especially if the parents are not observant or if they take obvious symptoms for granted

The following could indicate the sexual abuse of a child or an adolescent:

- Changes in eating pattern—self starvation or over eating
- Loss of interest in things that were previously considered as interesting
- Physical injuries on any part of the body
- Somatic effects such as headaches, muscular tension, gastrointestinal problems

- Bruises around the genital areas
- Sudden withdrawal
- Decreased academic performance which is not due to any other factor
- Substance abuse—alcohol, cigarette or other drugs
- Changes in sleeping pattern—insomnia (inability to sleep), narcolepsy (sleeping excessively)
- Loss of concentration
- Irrational fear and avoidance of certain places, events or persons
- Mood swings
- Anger outburst and hostility
- Crying or shedding tears without obvious reasons
- Torn clothes
- Blood stained clothes or beddings
- Possession of pornographic materials
- Age inappropriate knowledge or talk about sexual activities
- Hyper vigilance (increased alertness)
- Grief
- Forgetfulness
- Dissociation
- Depression
- Nightmares
- Self-neglect
- Excessive preoccupation with personal grooming—This can only occur where the abuse involves persuasion and reward.

If a child exhibits any of these behaviours, steps should be taken to investigate the actual cause of such a behavior. The easiest way to obtain information from a child is to approach the child in a manner that portrays affection, friendship, love, care and genuine concern.

Sometimes it could be helpful to talk with the child's friends, teachers or other close associates as they may have clues to what is happening to the child.

It is extremely dangerous for us to observe a strange behavior in our children and not show any concern. However, we need to avoid the mistake of drawing conclusion without proper investigation and confirmation of our suspicions.

Professional assistance such as the services of a counsellor or a child psychologist may be required for proper investigation.

HOW CAN A VICTIM BE HELPED?

Anyone who has been sexually abused needs help. Besides the physiological damage, it is difficult for a victim to single handedly resolve the psychological and emotional complications of sexual abuse. When the victim is a child, the situation becomes particularly difficult because as she has naturally not acquired the ability to deal with life problems rationally and effectively, hence she needs help as soon as possible. In order to effectively help a victim of sexual abuse, the assistance rendered must be multi-dimensional and should include the following:

- Medical assistance
- Psychotherapy (psychological assistance)
- Spiritual assistance

Medical Assistance—A victim requires urgent medical assistance in order to sort out the physiological problems that could result from sexual abuse such as pregnancy, STDs, and physical injuries. It is therefore recommended for a girl to see a doctor immediately after an abuse.

Psychotherapy—The kind of psychological assistance given to a victim of sexual abuse depends on the time of the intervention (whether it is immediately or long after the abuse) and the severity of the victim's psychological and emotional situation. If the abuse is detected immediately and the victim is given the needed professional psychological support probably by a counsellor, the victim's ability to cope with the abuse is enhanced and she may not need a clinical admission but if the victim does not get immediate assistance, and she develops a clinical condition such as PTSD, she will in addition to counseling require clinical therapy. It is important to point out that it is not all counsellors that can handle cases of trauma. **A counselor who is helping a traumatized victim of sexual abuse would need to refer the victim to a trauma specialist for proper assessment and management unless she is also professionally competent to manage trauma.**

The aim of the psychological support given to the victim is to provide rehabilitation, so that she would be able to resume normal life and functioning either as a student or as an income earner. Specifically, the objectives are:

- To help the victim to unburden, by prompting her to share her experience in an atmosphere of warmth, unconditional acceptance and empathy, so that she would be able to fully let out deep seated bitterness, hurt and grief, by giving full expression to them. The victim may shed tears, cry or laugh or even go into hysterics. Therapy will have no significant effect unless the victim has fully unburdened.
- To help her to resolve the emotional and psychological problems which could emanate from the abuse such as distorted self esteem, anxiety, insomnia, guilt, self pity and depression.
- To help her to achieve social integration. Here, the counselor helps the victim with social and emotional skills which will enable her to reintegrate. Such skills include the ability to forgive the offender, self acceptance, a positive attitude towards people rather than being suspicious of everyone, willingness to accept affection and love as well as the courage to interact without the fear of being abused.
- To reassure the victim of the wholeness and integrity of her person.
- Counseling will also focus on how to help the child to cope with the sexual urge which the abuse may have aroused especially for a child who has not attained adolescence, an example is the case of the 8years old girl discussed earlier, or an adolescent who was not sexually active before the abuse.

Spiritual Assistance

From the spiritual point of view, sexual abuse can impair the victim's belief and faith. I have seen people who were very religious prior to an abuse, become disoriented after the abuse. *"I don't think that God loves me enough to protect me"*, those were the words of a victim. A victim may begin to question the love and protection of God. Many victims feel that God must be unmindful of them for Him to have allowed such an event to occur in their lives. They may reduce their involvement in religious activities or stop entirely. They often feel betrayed by God. The more religious the individual was before the abuse, the more severe the spiritual disconnection would be.

It would therefore be helpful to provide a kind of spiritual re orientation to help the victim to reconsider her relationship with God. One of the things that will aid spiritual healing is the victim's ability to forgive the abuser, not necessarily because the abuser deserves her forgiveness but because she needs a clear conscience to relate freely with God. It is important to note that forgiveness is also an emotional therapy. It is impossible to achieve spiritual and emotional healing unless we forgive those who hurt us.

WHAT ELSE CAN PARENTS DO TO HELP?

While the medical, psychological and spiritual assistance would require the services of specialists in those fields, there are a few things which parents can do to help.

i. Be observant and take note of strange behaviours

ii. Do not take obvious symptoms for granted, ask questions and investigate strange behaviors, with expression of affection, concern and love.

iii. Seek professional help for proper investigation if you are in doubt of your findings, and for treatment if it is confirmed that the child has suffered an abuse.

iv. Go out of your way to show acceptance, understanding and love towards the child.

v. Apologize to the child if you feel that you have contributed either through negligence or otherwise to the abuse.

vi. Maintain confidentiality. Do not forget that what has happened to the child is sensitive and private, the more it is publicized, the more the child will feel stigmatized. Even when legal redress is sought, you need profession advice or the child's opinion (in the case of an adolescent) regarding the level of publicity that should be involved.

vii. Avoid ridicule, embarrassment, criticism or blaming of the incident on the child. Even if you think she contributed to the abuse, the fact remains that she is a victim; she needs empathy and not evaluation and condemnation.

viii. Help her to recover her self esteem and self confidence.

ix. Provide opportunities for her to laugh and have fun. This will help her to cushion the depressive effect of the abuse.

x. Discourage the use of drugs and alcohol as escape channels.

xi. Constantly reassure the child of your acceptance, appreciation, support, and unconditional love.

xii. Always ask the child if there is anything she would like you to do that will aid the process of recovery. For instance, a victim may request to be taken away from her immediate environment, especially if the abuser lives there or if the abuse took place in that environment.

xiii. Prevent subsequent abuse. Sometimes a child may be abused severally either by the same person or different persons. A single case of abuse is bad enough, but for a parent to allow a repetition of such an experience is a homicide.

xiv. Pray for the child. Many victims have found succour in the divine healing offered by religion. The victim needs to be encouraged to trust God for perfect healing and restoration.

CHAPTER FOUR

RISKY SEXUAL BEHAVIORS AMONG YOUNG PEOPLE.

How Involved are today's Young People?

To say that today's young people are grossly involved in sexual activities will be stating the obvious. Every academic year, many female students drop out of school as a result of unplanned pregnancies. Abandoned babies, street children and baby parents have increased in number.

A study shows that 70% of male and 50% of female Nigerian adolescents in secondary school have had sexual intercourse at least once. Out of the sexually active female adolescents, 21% had sex before the age of 15, 67% had been pregnant at least once, while 30.2% admitted to illegally induced abortion.

(Youth care project, 2010.)

As at 2001, 11.8million young people aged (15-24 years) were living with HIV globally, with 73% (8,614,000) of this burden resting on Africa. As at 2008, the same age bracket formed 45% of the global annual new infection of 2.7million. Each day, about 6000 young people become infected with HIV worldwide. Presently, sub-Saharan Africa constitutes 90% of the global figure of children under 15years who are living with HIV out of which 93,000 children are Nigerians. Meanwhile, it has been found that sexual intercourse accounts for about 80% of HIV infections in Africa.

(The NYSC Reproductive Health and HIV/AIDs Prevention Project Manual for Peer Educators, 2003.)

Besides sexual intercourse, many young people indulge in other indecent and harmful behaviors such as same sex relationship (lesbianism and gay relationship) sexual bullying and harassment, promiscuity, prostitution, strip dancing, masturbation, telephone sex, pornography, orgy, gang sex, internet dating and incest.

SAME SEX RELATIONSHIP, A DISTURBING REALITY.

A same sex relationship refers to a sexual relationship which occurs between two or more people of the same sex. Males who indulge in this kind of relationship are said to be gay while the females are referred to as lesbians. Sexual relationship between persons of the same sex is not only condemned by religion but also socially offensive. There had been suggestions that males who engage in homosexual relations may be at higher risk of contracting HIV/AIDS. Also, individuals who indulge in same sex relationship may become uninterested in persons of the opposite sex and this can generate serious problems in future mate selection and family life.

HOW DO YOUNG PEOPLE BECOME INVOLVED IN SAME SEX RELATIONSHIP?

Young people become involved in same sex relationship due to several risk factors. Children who are in the boarding and those who attend single sex schools are very much at risk. This is so because those who have been sexually active, but are now deprived of opportunities for sexual gratification may resort to same sex relationship as an alternative source of sexual gratification. When this happens, the innocent ones often become toys in the hands of the experienced ones.

Other children who are vulnerable to same sex relationship are those who are being raised by over-restrictive parents. How? Adolescence comes with sexual maturity, awareness, desire, attraction to the opposite sex, and a yearning to interact with, and be appreciated by people of the opposite sex. As young people of the opposite sex socialize with one another; expressing admiration and appreciation towards one another, they enjoy some form of emotional satisfaction even though such interactions may not necessarily involve physical intimacy.

When this opportunity to interact with the opposite sex is absent as a result of parental restriction, the tendency is for these young people to develop such romantic relationship with people of the same sex from whom they are not restricted.

Also, some young people often become desperate to explore their newly acquired sexual capabilities. When such persons cannot find the natural opportunities to achieve their sexual goals due to parental restrictions, they may want to try same sex relationship, since parents usually do not restrict their wards from peers of the same sex.

Hence, when we deprive our adolescents of interaction with their peers of the opposite sex, we indirectly expose them to worse dangers than those we are trying to prevent.

Equally vulnerable are hermaphrodites (persons who have both male and female sexual organs) and people who are trans-sexual (those who have the physiological characteristics of a particular sex, but feel they belong to the opposite sex and therefore want to dress and behave like people of the opposite sex, including those who have had a medical operation to change their sexual organs).

An individual, who has been sexually abused by someone of the opposite sex, may generalize their resentment to people of the opposite sex, such that all people of the opposite sex become unattractive. The individual may, as a result, begin to develop sexual attraction towards persons of the same sex. Relatedly, if someone was continuously sexually abused during childhood by someone of the same sex, especially if the abuse involved persuasion or seduction, in which case the child was positively reinforced, he/she may become conditioned to that kind of relationship to the point that it becomes preferable.

Also, a boy or a girl who is materialistic can easily be lured by rich lesbians or gay men into same sex relationship.

With this development, it is no longer very safe to go to bed just because your child is with someone of the same sex, unless you are sure of your child's safety.

SEXUAL BULLYING

Sexual bullying involves the use of one's strength or power to compel another to participate in a sexual activity. A lot of adolescent boys are involved in sexual bullying, especially those who abuse alcohol or other drugs and those who are involved in cult activities. Such boys do not believe that they need to persuade a girl to grant her consent to sexual activity because they feel they can take it by force.

Sexual bullying may involve beating or threatening the victim with a gun, a knife, acid or other dangerous weapons in order to compel her to comply with the sexual wishes of the assailant. Sometimes the assailant's weapon may not be physical; it could be a special position or power. For instance, a teacher may threaten his student with failure or low grades, and a boss may use his influence as a weapon against his subordinate.

Sexual bullying may take the form of rape, an attempted rape, or other unauthorized physical contacts.

RAPE AND TYPES OF RAPE.

As discussed earlier, rape is defined by the section 357 of the Nigerian criminal code as "having unlawful carnal knowledge of a woman or a girl without her consent, or with her consent if the consent is obtained by force or by means of threat or intimidation of any kind or by fear of harm or by means of false and fraudulent representation as to the nature of the act or in the case of a married woman, by impersonating her husband".

The section 214-225 of the criminal code prescribes up to 14years and even a life jail for sexual offences against minors.

The types of rape include:

Single Rape—the rape of a girl by a single man.

Gang Rape—the rape of a girl by two or more men or the rape of a group of girls by a group of men.

Date rape—the rape of a girl by a man with whom she is on a date.

Some boys are fond of adding sedatives to drinks which they offer to their 'dates', with the intention of having sexual intercourse with them while they are under the influence of such sedatives. Also, a group of boys may organize a party with the hidden motive of getting the female participants involved in sexual activities.

Often, we parents are only concerned with the protection of our children, but we do not care if our children abuse others.

"Boy 16, rapes nine year old in Mission house." This was the headline in the Nov 6, 2010 issue of the Saturday punch. It was the story of a 16year old boy who raped a nine year old girl on her way home from school at Adekile area of Ibadan, Oyo state.

Who are the rapists? This is a question we need to ask ourselves. Certainly, the rapists are not spirits; they are our sons and siblings. As much as we need to protect our wards against sexual abuse, we must also ensure that they do not abuse others.

WHAT IS SEXUAL HARASSMENT?

Sexual harassment involves behaviors that directly or indirectly put sexual pressure on another.

Sexual harassment could be verbal such as outright sexual solicitation, rude comments about the sexual appeal of an individual or verbal expression of imagined sexual relations with an individual, whether such expressions are made directly or through text messages, e-mails or phone calls.

Sexual harassment could also take non-verbal forms such as indecent exposure of one's body to an opposite sex, sending of pornographic materials to someone and seductive postures.

Although sexual harassment may not necessarily involve physical assault, yet, it assaults the victim emotionally.

Concerning sexual harassment, the majority of today's young girls are as culpable as their male counterparts. Many of them indulge in indecent body exposure under the guise of fashion. Indecent posture is also another issue. We were trained as young ladies to sit with our legs either crossed or closed, but that is no longer the culture. It is common these days to find ladies sit in public places without any regard for decency. While some ladies deliberately indulge in these indecent behaviors to harass men, others ignorantly indulge in them.

Whether we accept it or not, sexual harassment of males by females could lead to high incidence of rape. This is not to say that any man has the right to sexually assault a woman just because she is indecently dressed, rather, it is to point out the fact that men (by nature) are easily aroused by what they see, and that the majority of them lack the ability to exercise self control once they are aroused.

> *"And it came to pass in the evening that David arose from off his bed and walked upon the roof of the king's house and from the roof, he saw a woman washing herself and the woman was very beautiful to look upon. And David sent messengers and took her and she came unto him and he laid with her"* II Sam. 11:2&4

Though the woman did not deliberately expose herself, the king was aroused. What he saw led to his thoughts, imaginations and consequently his action. We have a duty to let our wards know that when they harass others, they put both themselves and their victims at risk of STDs and other consequences.

Adolescent boys also harass girls sexually. There had been cases where boys would send nude photographs of themselves or of other males or photographs of sexual scenes to girls.

PROMISCUITY IS BECOMING A NORM

An individual is said to be promiscuous if they keep multiple sexual partners. Some adolescents are not only involved in pre-marital sexual activities; they are equally involved with several partners at the same time. If sexual involvement with one partner is harmful enough for a young person, then it is definitely more destructive to be involved with multiple partners.

PROSTITUTION IS NOW MORE SOPHISTICATED

Prostitution simply means the exchange of sexual gratification for reward. The reward could be money, jewelry, house, good grades at school, an employment, a contract or a promotion. The truth is that a lot of girls in today's society are engaged in different forms of sex trade. Whether a girl operates in a room in a brothel, stands by the road, or keeps only one married man or a handful of familiar single men, as long as she does so for a reward, she is a prostitute. It makes no difference whether actual sexual intercourse is involved or whether she only poses nude or massages a man's body or allows him to fondle with hers. Prostitutes now have managers who mediate between them and prospective customers.

Another form of prostitution is internet prostitution—where a lady advertises herself for sex on the net. Young boys have also become involved in prostitution. It is becoming a norm for boys to date older and wealthier ladies.

What about strip dancing?

Strip dancing is another form of prostitution; it involves dancing nude to entertain others for money. Many nightclubs have been reported to host strip dancing. Besides the dance, any spectator who feels thrilled by the lady's body and can afford the fee may take her away.

The Desperation To Live Abroad Has Landed Many Young Girls In Sex Trade.

In 2009, about 10,000 Nigerian girls were found stranded in Libya and Morocco. In 2010, the National Agency for the Prohibition of Trafficking in Persons (NAPTIP) noted that between 20,000 and 40,000 Nigerian women and girls were found in brothels in Mali. At least, 60% of foreign prostitutes in Italy are said to be from African countries with most of them coming from Nigeria. *(Sunday Punch. Nov. 14, 2010)*

Why is your daughter travelling abroad, why do you really want her to travel? What provisions have you made to ensure her wellbeing over there?

The pressure to achieve has driven many of our young ones into catastrophe.

We do not need to pressurize our children to achieve, if we encourage hard work and integrity, they will always succeed.

HOW IS MASTURBATION HARMFUL?

Masturbation is the act of manipulating one's own genitals for the purpose of sexual gratification. Young people who indulge in masturbation may experience difficulty in future family life because there is the tendency for them to neglect the sexual needs of their spouses since they are capable of providing sexual satisfaction for themselves. Another harm is that among many adolescents who masturbate, an imaginary sexual partner often accompanies the act. This means that the adolescent is abstractly with an opposite sex, even though he/she is alone physically.

Many children and adolescents already know that masturbation is improper. Hence, they often experience guilt and consequent depression after the act.

THAT PARTY COULD BE AN ORGY

An orgy is a party where there is a lot of eating, drinking, pornography and sexual activities. You may call it a sex party. The sex partners may be familiar mates or complete strangers who are meeting for the first time at the party. Under the influence of drugs and alcohol which are common features of such parties, it is unrealistic to think that the participants would insist on any form of protection against STDs and pregnancy. It sounds crazy and unbelievable, but it is a reality. **What kind of parties does your child attend?**

Pornography Exposes Children to Early Sexual Activity.

A child that is exposed to pornography is likely to experiment with sex early. What we see affects our thoughts and our thoughts influence our behaviours. A child or an adolescent who is pre-occupied with sexual images is likely to think often about sexual intercourse and also fantasize about it. Hence, he or she is likely to experiment with sexual activities.

How Safe is Internet Dating for Minors?

There is no doubt that the internet offers awesome educational and economic opportunities for young people. Nevertheless, it has also launched a major attack on the sexual responsibility of today's young people. The internet makes it possible for children to date without parents' suspicion. Besides the fact that children may be unduly exposed to countless strangers on the dating site, other harmful characteristics of internet dating include exposure to pornographic images and sexual solicitations. Another negative feature of internet dating is imaginary sex, which is commonly referred to as telephone sex. The act involves the parties guiding each other to masturbate through the telephone while imagining that they are physically together.

From the moral point of view, imaginary sex is not in anyway different from actual sexual intercourse.

Internet dating does not begin and end on the internet, after a while, the relationship is often transformed into an off-line reality.

In a study carried out by Barbovschi (2009), on internet dating involving 2,000 adolescents, she found that 60% of the sample reported at least one exposure to pornographic images online, while 5% declared that they had been exposed to sexual solicitations online. She asserted that internet dating exposes children to early sexual activity. Internet dating has been blamed for early experimentation of sexual intercourse among adolescents. (Davis and Banserman, 1993). *Do you know what your child does online?*

HOW WOULD I KNOW IF MY CHILD IS INVOLVED IN A RISKY SEXUAL BEHAVIOR?

If you are close to your child and also observant, it will not be difficult to discern when things go wrong with your child. However, the following behaviours may signify danger:

1. Unreasonable demand for privacy which outweighs adolescents' normal craving for privacy.
2. Expression of age inappropriate sexual knowledge.
3. Going out without permission or against warning.

4. Spending more time than necessary on errands.
5. Leaving too early for school or coming back late.
6. Sneaking out of the room or house at nights.
7. Loss of enthusiasm.
8. Loss of interest in activities which were previously interesting to the child.
9. Possession of sex toys
10. Change in sleeping pattern.
11. Possession of more money than what is given by the parents.
12. Coming home with gifts.
13. Late night calls and night browsing.
14. Substance abuse (Drinking of alcohol, smoking or taking of drugs).
15. Reduction in the time spent with the family.
16. Dwindling grades which cannot be traced to other factors.
17. Unusual laziness and procrastination.
18. Truancy.
19. Self isolation and withdrawal.
20. Depression.
21. Unusual hostility.
22. Unusual calmness or elation without apparent reasons.
23. Expression of feminine behaviours (if a boy) or masculine behaviors (if a girl).
24. Possession of pornographic materials.
25. Possession of contraceptive devices.
26. Indecent dressing.
27. Making friends with people who have questionable life styles.
28. Avoidance of eye contact and interrogation.
29. A sudden surge in grades which is not the result of effort.
30. Absent mindedness and forgetfulness.
31. Loss of interest in religious activities.
32. Excessive preoccupation with personal grooming.
33. Sleeping out.

While these behaviors may not automatically indicate a child's involvement in risky sexual behaviours, they could be pointers to other hidden problems. Hence, you need to investigate, if you observe any of these behaviours in your child or adolescent.

HOW DOES SEXUAL IRRESPONSIBILITY AFFECT YOUNG PEOPLE, THEIR FAMILIES AND THE SOCIETY?

The devastating consequences of unwholesome sexual behaviors on young people include:

- ➤ The risk of becoming a drop-out due to an unplanned pregnancy.
- ➤ Dwindling academic performance as a result of inhibited concentration.
- ➤ Unplanned pregnancy.
- ➤ Future sterility resulting from prolonged use of contraceptives or damaged reproductive organs which could result from abortions.
- ➤ Pregnancy complications e.g. Vesicle Vagina Fistula (VVF) which could result from early sexual experimentation and teenage pregnancy.
- ➤ Sexually transmitted diseases such as HIV/AIDS, Chlamydia, Syphilis, Gonorrhea, Genital Warts, Pelvic Inflammatory Disease (PID) and Herpes.
- ➤ Infant and maternal mortality.
- ➤ Spiritual alienation.
- ➤ Painful emotional consequences such as shame, guilt, anxiety, depression and suicide attempts in some cases.
- ➤ Involvement in sexual activities at the expense of educational and career development can mar the individual's future economically.
- ➤ Early sexual activity and promiscuity have been found to be high risk factors for cervical cancer.

When a Young Person Suffers, the Family Inevitably Suffers.

Besides the social, emotional and psychological consequences of having an irresponsible ward, the family may also have to expend huge sums of money on medical care if the young person contracts STDs. If a child results, the family will have an additional member to cater for. Also, the young person whose educational development has been disrupted by an unplanned pregnancy becomes a clog in the wheel of the family's economic progress.

How is the Society Affected?

An increase in the number of drop outs, emotionally disturbed and disease infested young people only spells a bleak future for the society. Besides the fact that these incapacitated young people would not be able to contribute adequately to societal development, those who are infected with STDs will constitute public health problems for the society and consequently increase government expenditure on health.

Also, children who are born to baby parents often suffer from inadequate parenting, and in many cases turn out to be delinquent and constitute social and economic nuisance.

HOW CAN I HELP A CHILD WHO IS ALREADY INVOLVED?

Consider the following:

1. Express unconditional love and acceptance towards the child. The easiest way to make change difficult for a child that has a behavioural problem is to make them feel unwanted.
2. Initiate an intimate friendship with the child. You can only make meaningful impact on a child who is close to you and believes in you.
3. Reassure the child of their worth and dignity. It is very difficult for people to change once they believe that they have already lost everything (due to their behavior) and therefore have nothing left to protect. Let the child know that his/her worth and dignity as a human being and as a member of the family are still intact. This will help the child to deal with possible feelings of inferiority and encourage them to work towards positive change in order to recover their lost reputation.
4. Avoid criticism, ridicule and condemnation. When we criticize people, they become defensive and focus more on how to justify their behaviors, and therefore, focus less on "change". On the contrary, when we refuse to criticize them, especially when they expect us to do so, we give them the opportunity to reflect on their behaviours.
5. Assess your parental involvement objectively, and own up to your parental inadequacies which may have contributed to the problem, apologize to the child and be ready to make amendment. The truth is that our children pick up unpleasant behaviours either because of the things we do or those we fail to do.
6. Discuss the behavior plainly and in details with your child in a manner that is neither evaluative nor judgmental. Let the child tell you when and how the behavior started and how it has been perpetrated. You

also need to find out the situations or circumstances that usually prompt the child to exhibit the behavior. All these will enable you to ascertain the causes, the severity of the problem as well as the factors which reinforce the behavior.

7. Motivate and encourage the child to see the need for a positive change. Discuss the benefits of a positive change as well as the consequences of failure to change.

8. Facilitate positive change—Based on the data gathered in No. 6 above, take practical steps to help the child to achieve change. For instance, a boy who masturbates may be prompted to do so after an exposure to pornographic materials, a practical step could be to encourage him to do away with such materials.

9. Assist the child to explore productive ways of expending his youthful energy—music, sports, writing and religious activities.

10. Seek professional help if you cannot handle the situation.

11. I personally believe that our efforts will always yield better results, when they are combined with prayers. Do you believe? If you do, then pray for the child.

CHAPTER FIVE

62 WAYS YOUNG PEOPLE ARE EXPOSED TO SEXUAL ABUSE AND RISKY SEXUAL BEHAVIORS

The situations that expose children and adolescents to sexual abuse and harmful sexual behaviours can be classified into:

- Ways they are exposed by their parents.
- Ways they are inherently vulnerable.
- Ways they are exposed by the school.
- Ways they are exposed by the society.

WAYS PARENTS EXPOSE YOUNG PEOPLE TO SEXUAL ABUSE AND RISKY SEXUAL BEHAVIORS:

1. Keeping other grown-ups in the same apartment with your children is a direct exposure.
2. When you allow your grown ups to bring their lovers home in your absence, the little ones play the audience to their romantic activities.
3. When you hide pornographic materials in your home, you can be sure that your little ones know where they are.
4. When you lock a child out of the home you cannot guarantee what happens to the child.
5. When you fail to provide adequately for your children, you are asking them to look for other sources of survival, their benefactors may take advantage of them.
6. Child labour—Giving children out as domestic servants or making them to hawk about exposes them.

7. If we fail to show interest in whom our children keep as friends, we should not be surprised if they come up with embarrassing behaviours.
8. When we allow under aged children to go about without an adult company, we expose them to predators.
9. Leaving children in school after closing hours makes them available to predators.
10. When we send our adolescents abroad without adequate provision for their wellbeing, we license them to prostitute.
11. When you deny your child of the needed parental affection and emotional support, you are driving them into the arms of someone else.
12. If you fail to supervise the relationship between your child and a step parent of the opposite sex, you are taking a serious risk.
13. When you place unbearable financial pressure on your working adolescent, you are pushing her into prostitution.
14. When you pressurize your schooling daughter to achieve grades which her aptitude and efforts cannot earn, you are telling her to trade her body for such grades.
15. If your child reports a case of sexual harassment and you shun her or do nothing about it, she may end up being abused.
16. When you implant low self esteem in your child, you make them vulnerable to emotional manipulation and consequently sexual abuse.
17. If you are not your child's friend, she is unlikely to discuss issues that bother on sexuality with you. She would not tell you when someone is making passes at her.
18. Parents who over restrict their adolescents from social relations encourage incest without knowing it.
19. Where there are no family values and ideals or where they are not enforced, waywardness is inevitable.
20. When the home is not conducive for the emotional wellbeing of the children as it is in broken and dysfunctional homes, they are bound to seek succour outside the home and this makes them vulnerable.
21. When we allow our adolescents to work in high risk environments such as bars and hotels, we expose them to sexual immorality.
22. If as a single mother, you often send your daughter to your male friend, you shouldn't be surprised if you find out that your friend has been sleeping with your daughter.
23. When your children discover that you are keeping extra marital affair, what you are preaching is that it is okay to be sexually immoral.
24. When the houseboy and house girl play their game, the children play the audience.

25. When parents fail to exercise caution in the way they go about their romance, especially when they let their children see or hear them, they send a negative signal to the children that **"what is happening between mum and dad needs to be tried out"**. There is nothing wrong with a warm embrace of your spouse, a welcome or a goodbye peck in the presence of the children, but all the "necking" we do in their presence is simply unnecessary.

26. When we send our adolescents to get our contraceptives, what we are telling them is that they can have sex and go scot-free.

27. When we watch a movie together with our children, and ignore the romantic scenes or simply skip over them instead of giving proper explanation and guidance, we leave them in doubt and confusion about the appropriateness or otherwise of such scenes.

28. When older ones send love messages through the little ones, they place them (the little ones) under apprenticeship.

29. When we allow children of the opposite sex to use the bath or convenience together without adult supervision, we create an atmosphere for them to explore their genitals.

30. When we leave children without supervision, we let them experiment with everything including their genitals.

31. When we fail to give our children appropriate sexuality information, we allow them to be destroyed by their ignorance.

32. If all a child is made to see about the future is hopelessness and mediocrity, there is a tendency for her to be wayward because she has nothing to live for.

33. If we fail to assist our children to coin out worthy goals, ideals, values and personal philosophies, they will live their lives without positive drives and without direction.

34. When you send your daughter to a man to beg for favors, you can be sure that she is paying for such favors.

Certain conditions, traits and behaviours make some young people more vulnerable:

35. Indecent dressing.

36. Children who attain puberty very early are confronted by sexual advances at an age when they are not intellectually mature enough to discern and avoid danger.

37. Indulgence in alcohol and drugs—It is difficult to enforce personal values when under the influence of alcohol or drugs.

38. Any girl who goes out indiscriminately is likely to be abused often.

39. Laziness—Any girl who wants to have the best of things without working hard to acquire them is likely to trade her body for such things.
40. A young person who lacks worthwhile goals will also lack focus and inevitably settle for waywardness.
41. When an individual lacks self-control, immediate gratification becomes a life style.
42. Greed, materialism and ostentatious lifestyle—Anyone who is desperate for material possessions would do anything to get them.
43. A lady who has low self esteem is an easy prey for manipulators.
44. Many young people are ignorant of the consequences of harmful sexual behaviors.
45. Some young people are not willing to learn—Anyone who does not listen to good counsel will definitely end up badly.
46. The inability to channel youthful energy into productive activities has made many young people to adopt sex as a recreational activity.
47. Lack of psychological independence makes one vulnerable to negative peer influence and manipulation.
48. An untreated early sexual abuse—One of the consequences of early sexual abuse is that the child may grow up to become sexually irresponsible, especially if the abuse was not properly treated.
49. Predators can easily manipulate a child that is mentally challenged.
50. A girl who lacks assertiveness can easily be intimidated.
51. Children who are very inquisitive and adventurous naturally like to try out things, they can easily get into trouble if they are not well informed and adequately supervised.
52. A young person who lacks personal identity and values can easily be influenced or enticed.

Many Schools are Culpable.

53. In many cities in Nigeria, school children spend an average of eight hours daily within the school premises. During this period, the teachers are expected to be surrogate parents to these children, by offering physical protection and supervision of their activities. On the contrary, many teachers are incompetent to play this role. There have been cases of sexual molestation of school children by their mates during school hours. It is common to find school children within the school premises after closing hours without adult supervision.
54. Some young teachers exchange love notes through their students.
55. Some teachers molest their students sexually.
56. Some nursery school teachers encourage both boys and girls to use the convenience together. Research has shown that some of these

innocent children sometimes explore one another's genitals, unaware of the implications of their actions.

57. The majority of the administrators of today's boarding schools lack the necessary competence. There have been cases of students being initiated into lesbianism and gay relationships by older boarders. Students sneak out to attend night parties. To the utmost disappointment of parents, many children have left their homes as virgins only to return with sexual experience.

58. Many schools fail to provide sexuality education for their students and the few who attempt to do so have no formal curriculum for it. The most fundamental of these problems is that many schools do not have qualified counselors, therefore, they have nothing to offer to their students in terms of guidance and moral training.

Today's Youngsters are Victims of Societal Irresponsibility

59. Today's society lacks role models for the young ones to emulate. It is common to find a man in his 50s keeping a sexual relationship with a teenage girl.

60. We have completely lost our values, we now perceive chastity as a primitive virtue—instead of guiding and motivating our young ones to uphold abstinence, we are teaching them safe sex. Marital infidelity is common in our society today. If we who are married cannot restrict our sexual appetites, what moral justification do we have to teach our young ones about self-control?

61. Many employers would not employ a female without a bedroom interview.

62. The contemporary media is another snare to today's young people; movies with sexually explicit messages are freely broadcast on TV even during the waking hours of children. Not withstanding its educational and economic advantages, the internet has impacted negatively on the sexual sanity of today's young people.

CHAPTER SIX

HOW TO PROTECT YOUR WARDS AGAINST SEXUAL ABUSE AND RISKY SEXUAL BEHAVIOURS

55 WAYS TO PROTECT YOUR WARDS AGAINST SEXUAL ABUSE AND RISKY SEXUAL BEHAVIORS?

It is easier and cheaper to prevent a problem than to solve it. The following tips may be helpful.

1. Make adequate provision for the child, especially food, clothing, shelter and education.
2. Teach contentment early enough.
3. Adequate supervision of children is inevitable. If you would not be around, you should delegate a responsible adult to do it.
4. It is safer not to keep outsiders or distant relatives in your home, but if you must keep them, you must ensure that they are morally sound.
5. Children need to be taught to define their personal boundaries with the opposite sex irrespective of whether they are friends or relatives.
6. Being clear and firm on issues of physical boundaries between your child and any opposite sex who lives in your home is a good warning signal to that person. For instance, if you do not allow your male relation to carry your 7years old daughter on his laps, he may not attempt it in your absence. Also, if you forbid him from entering into her room, he may not have the courage to do so in your absence.
7. You need to know what literature your child is reading, what music he is listening to, what movies he is watching and what he does on the net so that you can make necessary input.

8. It is important to know who your child's friends are so that you can guide him/her accordingly. Encourage your children especially the adolescents to bring their friends home because you cannot know if they are good or bad unless you know them and interact with them.

9. Do not encourage your grown ups who are in relationships to bring their lovers home in your absence. It is safer when you are present.

10. Train your little girl not to sit on people's labs or let them toy with her body.

11. Take advantage of every opportunity to provide sexuality information for your child. For instance, if you are watching a movie together with your child and a couple begin to kiss, do not skip over, look away or ask the child to leave, rather let them know that kissing is only appropriate for married people. Also, let them know what could go wrong if unmarried people indulge in such an act. Give the age appropriate sexuality information on time.

The only way to prevent your child from being misled or deceived is to tell them the truth before a stranger tells them a lie.

12. Being close to your child makes it easy for you to discern when trouble approaches so that you can provide the appropriate intervention before it becomes too late.

13. Teach them how to identify predators and how to avoid them.

14. If you are a single parent, keep your child out of your relationship with the opposite sex.

15. Show good examples, be a model of positive values to your child.

16. Let your house help and other grown ups who live in your house know your position on indecent behaviours.

17. Discuss issues openly and freely with your children especially adolescents. Talk about incest, masturbation, premarital sex, rape, internet dating, romance and the consequences of indulgence. If you feel you cannot handle it, get a professional to do it. *Leaving children in ignorance is more destructive than protective.*

18. Set dating guidelines and discuss them with your adolescents.

19. Shield your children from your sex life.

20. Nurture your children with love, affection and appreciation. Let them be convinced about your unconditional love for them. Let them know that you will love them no matter what and that you will always be available.

21. Let your family life radiate acceptance, love and belongingness; do not let your children seek succour outside your home.

22. Be available to provide emotional support for your child. Show interest in the child's personal concerns and try to help no matter how trivial

such concerns may appear to be. Children also have moments of depression and would always appreciate support at such moments.

23. Do not over restrict your children from socializing with their peers and do not give them freedom without limits. For instance, you may let your adolescent visit his friend provided that you know the person, the place and that he does so within a specified period of time. You may take a step further to ensure that the friend's parents are at home to supervise them before you grant your permission.

24. Help your child to build their self-esteem so that they can develop self-respect.

25. Assist your child to set worthwhile values and goals, and focus on them in order to avoid distractions.

26. Teach your children time management skills. Let them know that waste of time is waste of life and that it makes no sense to spend valuable time on things that have no lasting benefits.

27. Never send your daughter to a man to ask for favors.

28. Teach them how to channel their youthful energies into productive use. They can achieve that by participating in sports, music, drama, drawing, painting, sculpture, writing, gardening and religious activities.

29. Be observant and do not take the obvious for granted. If you observe any strange behavior, the best thing to do is to ask questions or try to investigate such a behavior. It is dangerous to assume that all is well when there are obvious signs of danger.

30. Children with ambiguous genitalia should not be ignored; rather, medical solutions should be sought for them early enough.

31. Teach them to be assertive and to be courageous enough to defend their values and protect their rights.

32. Equip them with decision making skills—the ability to ponder and weigh consequences before making choices.

33. Any parent who knows how to discuss or dialogue would always achieve more with children and adolescents than the one who only knows how to 'preach'.

34. Set worthwhile family values and try to adhere to them. You may find it interesting to know that as corrupt as today's society is, some families still uphold chastity and transfer it from generation to generation.

35. Provide books and other learning aids which support positive values.

36. Teach children to learn self-control early enough, teach them to understand that there is honor in delaying gratification. Let them learn to be masters over their passions and impulses. Let them know that integrity begins with being able to rule oneself. *Let them know that the greatest power that man can ever possess, is not the might to subdue others, but the strength to rule himself.*

37. Learn to enforce discipline—set limits and boundaries and be firm on them.

38. It is not enough to preach abstinence, teach them how to avoid difficult situations and how abstinence can be made easy. Rules concerning not "pulling" "unbuttoning" and "unzipping" will not be necessary if young people learn to keep away from bad situations.

39. Teach them to dress decently and to comport themselves well.

40. Teach them to treasure and respect their bodies. Let them know the benefits of sexual purity.

41. Visit your child's school, find out if there are loopholes in the childcare system and make helpful suggestions to the management.

42. Provide good role models.

43. It is good to trust your child, but it is also good to verify that trust. If your working adolescent tells you that she is on a night shift, it would not be a waste of effort to verify that.

44. Children should be discouraged from accepting gifts from people because many people use gifts as baits to attract children for sexual abuse.

45. Do not pressurize your child to achieve. Ensure that your child has the intellectual ability to perform well in her field of study. Many young girls have become sex objects to their lecturers because of the pressure to achieve grades that they cannot ordinarily achieve.

46. Do not put financial burden on your working adolescents. Though they need to show some financial commitment to the family, unnecessary pressure will expose them to desperation and make them vulnerable

47. Do not jump at every opportunity to send your child abroad. Investigate and be sure of whom your child is traveling with and what she would be doing there. Keeping contact with the child while there is also crucial. Loss of contact with your child indicates danger.

48. We live, plan and thrive because we hope for a better future. Never allow your child to think there is no future for them. Always assure them that they have a great future ahead even though their present circumstances may be unfavorable. Hopelessness can lead to waywardness.

49. Drop and pick your child up from the school at the right time. Do not allow your child to remain in the school when others are gone.

50. Treating your child with dignity is the most effective way to enhance their self esteem. A child that is always made to feel worthless would also think that she has nothing worth protecting and would not learn to demand respect from others.

51. Teach hard work early enough and discourage laziness. Any girl that is lazy would more readily trade her body for the good things of life than the girl who knows that she can achieve anything by working hard.

52. Your response to your child's complaint about an on going sexual harassment can either deflate her confidence in your ability to protect her or reassure her of it. When a child reports a case of sexual harassment, she should be commended for having the courage to report. The case must be investigated, and the culprit (if found guilty) must be confronted.
53. Children should be taught early, not to undress in front of others.
54. Know when to seek help.
55. Pray for them and teach them the fear of God. Let children know early enough that they were created by God, and that they are to account for what they do with their time and bodies.

WHAT IS THE PLACE OF SPIRITUAL TRAINING?

"The fear of God is the beginning of wisdom" Prov. 1:7.

"Religion is the foundation of morality. Religious beliefs and practices provide stability and order. If there is anything that will stop people in the heat of passion, it is religious convictions. Many youth have been prevented from going all the way in the heat of passion by a troubled conscience that was sensitized by religious teachings". *(Prof. Danny Mc Cain, 2003).*

Teaching young people about God and encouraging them to develop an intimate personal relationship with him, is in my opinion, the most dependable solution to moral bankruptcy among young people.

The essence of spiritual training is to help the child to discover God through personal interaction with him (God). It is only when this is achieved that religious principles and values become "personalized" and "internalized".

When a young person has an intimate personal relationship with God, he will not only fear Him and shun evil, he will also thrive to please Him in all things. The spiritual training of children can neither be substituted by material provision nor formal education. The only way to be sure that your child would be upright even in your absence is to lead him to Christ.

CHAPTER SEVEN

QUESTIONS PARENTS ASK ABOUT YOUNG PEOPLE'S SEXUALITY

The scope of this book will not permit us to look into all the issues which parents often raise concerning children and adolescents' sexuality. Hence, we shall consider only the most crucial ones.

At what age should parents commence sexuality education for children and what are the guidelines?

Sexuality education does not begin with information about sexual intercourse, rather, it begins with teaching a child to treasure, respect and protect her body, and this can be taught as soon as the child is mature enough to understand spoken language. For instance, at the age of two, a female child can be taught to sit with her thighs closed. Both boys and girls at this age can be discouraged from toying with their genitals and they can also be taught not to undress in front of others.

The most fundamental part of sexuality education is teaching children to show respect for their bodies and other people's bodies. Unless this precept is set, subsequent training will be meaningless.

As children begin to learn about the different parts of the body, usually at the age of 3, they should be taught to use the right words for the genitals. Let them know that the vagina is called vagina and the penis is called penis. Teaching children to identify their genitals by funny names makes them to associate those parts of their bodies with "fun". The implication of this is that they grow up to see their genitals as objects which are meant for fun or pleasure, rather than for serious purposes, and this will have a negative impact on their attitude to sex as they grow up. It is also at this stage that children should be taught not to accept gifts from people without their parents' approval and not to allow people to toy with their bodies.

As from the age of 8, as children approach puberty, they should be told what to expect such as ovulation, menstruation, wet dreams, physical attractions and how to handle advances from the opposite sex. They should be taught about the benefits of abstinence as wall as the consequences of irresponsible sexual behaviours such as unplanned pregnancy, disruption in education and career, STDs, death.

The efficiency of any sexuality education program for children lies in knowing what to teach at a particular stage and how to teach it. You may employ the services of a counselor if you have difficulties in this area.

At what age should a boy/girl start dating?

The first step in answering this question is to clarify the meaning of the word "dating". Dating is the process of mate selection for the purpose of marriage. It is a not too intimate relationship in which two adults of the opposite sex who are attracted to each other meet regularly to assess their suitability for future marriage. If both parties are satisfied with their level of compatibility and how they complement each other, dating is said to be successful and will lead to engagement, courtship and eventual marriage.

Contrary to what many young people think, the above definition makes it clear that dating is a serious business that is neither for children nor for leisure. Besides age, other variables such as psychological independence, emotional maturity as well as economic independence need to be considered and all these may not be achieved until late adolescence (20-24yrs). A young person who is not ready for marriage should have no business with dating.

Should I teach my adolescent about contraceptives?

To conceal important information from your child is to let the child grope in ignorance and ignorance is the primary cause of vulnerability to sexual irresponsibility among young people.

Young people have the right to be informed so that they would not be misled.

Informing your child about contraceptives does not encourage irresponsibility, rather, it protects your child against being misled about them. Whether parents talk about contraceptives or not, an average adolescent already knows about them. It is therefore necessary for you as a parent to clarify the misconceptions which the child already has concerning them. These misconceptions include the belief that contraceptives are 100% effective and that condoms can prevent all kinds of sexually transmitted diseases.

Your child needs to know that in 1993, Susan Weller a Texas researcher evaluated all the researches conducted on condom effectiveness published before 1970, and reported that condoms are only 87% effective in preventing pregnancy and 67% effective in preventing HIV infection. This implies 13% failure in preventing pregnancy and 33% failure in preventing HIV. Your adolescent needs to know that condoms cannot prevent some STDs such as Syphilis, Genital warts, and Herpes because apart from sexual intercourse, they can also be contracted through intimate genital contact and kissing. Condoms cannot prevent the heartbreak that will result if a partner disappoints one after sexual involvement. Also, there is yet to be a single pill that is 100% reliable. Meanwhile, prolonged use of pills have been found to impair fertility.

Should parents encourage abortion?

According to medical experts, an abortion is only necessary when a woman's life is threatened by a pregnancy, in which case an abortion can only be recommended and carried out by a certified obstetrician. Some parents encourage abortion in order to avert the embarrassment which such pregnancies may bring to the family, while some argue that their young daughters' education may be jeopardized if such pregnancies are kept, but there are more crucial issues than shame and temporary disruption in education which need to be considered, such as possible abortion complications which could cause damage to the reproductive organs or death. The life of the unborn child is also important.

Children would never become responsible if parents continue to shield them from the consequences of their choices. To abort a pregnancy for a girl is to encourage promiscuity.

REFERENCES

Action Health Incorporated, (2002). Can we Really Talk About It? Lagos: Action Health Inc.

Ikulayo, B. P. (1999).Family Life and Sex Education. Lagos: Phil-chel Educational Consultancy Services.

Kirby, S. (2000). Dating-Guidelines from the Bible. Belarus: PrintCorp

Langberg, D.M. (1997). Counseling Survivors of Sexual Abuse. USA: Tyndale House Publishers, Inc.

Makinde, B. O. (2004). Human Sexuality Education and Marital Guidance. Lagos: Raytel Communications Ltd.

Odunukwe, T. N. (2010). Sexuality and You. Lagos: Royal Pat Associates

Osarenren, N. (2002). Child Development and Personity. Lagos: Derate Nigeria Limited.

Saliu, D.O. (2009). I Did not Ask For It. Benin city: Ambik Press Ltd

Stan and Brenna (1973). Facing the Facts—the Truth About Sex and You. USA: Navpress.

UNICEF (2003). NYSC Reproductive Health and HIV/AIDS Prevention Project Manual for Peer Educators. Abuja : UNICEF.